The Real Dope on Dealing with an Addict:

How Addiction Saved My Life

By Meridith Powell & Beth Brand

ISBN-10: 1469961776
ISBN-13: 9781469961774

For Cabell and the next generation

Contents

Part III — Managing Your Life

Part IV — Living

Preface:
Our Stories

Beth's Story

My earliest memories of my paternal grandfather are of a man in a pressed white shirt, cufflinks, tie, boxer shorts, and socks, running around his house, calling his wife, my sweet grandmother, the most distasteful of names.

He was an educated, extremely successful businessperson. He had done well by his family financially. My father had an undergraduate degree from Yale University and received his master's degree at Penn. My uncle was educated at George Washington University Medical School and was a physician in private practice. Both had attended prep school.

No one ever challenged my grandfather in my presence, criticized his behavior or said that his attire was unacceptable. No one shielded me from his tirades. No one ever said that the terrible name he used for my grandmother was offensive. No one ever mentioned to five-year-old, six-year-old or seven-year-old me that he was an alcoholic and that I should not depend on his judgment. In fact, my parents dropped me and my brother Ted off at my grandparent's house every Saturday to spend the night. My older brother, Larry, spent Friday nights with them.

My own home was nurturing and my parents intelligent, loving and respectful to each other during my early childhood. Surely they wouldn't leave me with someone who was unsafe. And so since no one told me otherwise, I did trust that my grandfather's behavior was normal and was to be tolerated.

In fairness, I guess my parents believed that my grandmother would protect my brothers and me from physical harm; she had after all protected my father and his brother, hadn't she. (My much younger sister Meridith, with whom I am writing this book, was never left with them — though she was not spared; little more than a decade later, she'd be left at home to deal with my father's descent into addiction.) But the reality was that my young brothers and I witnessed erratic behavior, rants against the world, horrible disrespect to others, and the buying of our love and forgiveness with new toys, donuts and rides to school. (All patterns that I would later tolerate from others in my life.) As children, we accepted it all — we accepted crazy — as normal. After all, our parents didn't say otherwise, and it was what we had known since infancy.

My grandfather died a sad, confused, but well-off alcoholic in his 90s. My father died of alcoholism at 57. My oldest brother was in his 40s when alcoholism took his life. My husband died of a morphine overdose at 42. My sister's husband died of alcoholism at 40. And my brother Ted killed himself at the age of 52 in May of 2011.

I don't tell you this to shock you or to blame my parents or my grandfather because I know that they have similar tales from their own childhoods. I tell you this to show you that **addiction is a disease** that doesn't die with the alcoholic. Allowed to fester in polite silence, it infects and takes down every member of the family in one way or another for generations. But dealt with head-on, addiction can take people to new levels of healthy living and healthy relationships.

Of course, getting to a place where you can deal with addiction honestly and openly is a trip in itself and one I have been on my whole life, most consciously in the last 15 years. Obviously, I have walked the road of addiction many times, at many stages of my life, in many different relationships. And I will tell you that I have no magic words to cure your addict or you (and yes, enablers are playing the game with as much commitment and craziness as the addicts). But what I do want to share with you is a wealth of practical knowledge that will clear your path so you can know what to expect, identify the red flags, have an action plan if you wish, and know who can and cannot help you when things spin out of control. And things will spin out of control.

My hope is that this information, which I so wish I had known decades ago, can free you from the details of addiction and eliminate some backward steps, so that you can take your recovery (yes, enablers need to recover too) as far as you can. Because it will be through your recovery that your addict's recovery is more likely, though not guaranteed. That is the hard truth. At the very least, a healthy you living fully and freely robs this disease of the silence it needs to thrive.

Your living in truth will be the miracle vaccine that protects and saves the next generation.

Meridith's Story

I make my living helping people understand the power and impor-
tance of communication and connection. Ironically, I have spent the
majority of my life avoiding both. I am the adult child of an alcoholic.
I love that term, because it so beautifully explains what happens to a
child raised in an alcoholic home. Certainly we grow up to be adults —
technically — but emotionally and spiritually we are stuck as children.
Until we understand the damage alcoholism brings into our lives, deal
with the lack of trust and anger that we feel, and take responsibility
for setting boundaries and making changes, we are stuck in the past,
stuck in our childhood.

I am what you would call an overachiever; I don't do anything half
way. My role as an enabler and child of an alcoholic is no exception.
While many of us suffer from alcoholism in our families, my family has
seen more than our fair share. To date, six male members of our family
have died from drinking themselves to death, and most recently my
brother committed suicide after struggling with this disease for more
than 30 years. While the male members of my family have excelled
at drinking, the females have excelled at the other half of this disease;
we are champion enablers. To be clear — we are all sick with some
form of the disease of addiction.

We were the perfect family. From the outside it all looked so right.
My father, a graduate of Yale and the University of Pennsylvania, was
a very successful businessman. My mother was a strikingly beautiful
woman with just the right balance of grace, brains and humor. Both
men and women admired her. My parents were in love, they wanted
a family, and they adored their children. There were four of us; again
just perfect, with two boys and two girls.

I was the youngest of the four children and had a different experience growing up than my brothers and my sister. They first encoun-
tered the addiction problems in our family through my grandparents.
My grandfather was a cruel man, who I would later learn was most
likely the source of my father's drinking. And my grandmother was the

champion of enablers. She vowed never to leave my grandfather, yet consistently begged everyone around her to save her from his cruelty.

Looking back, it is so easy for me to see now that my grandfather would serve as my both brothers' chief role model. My brothers both started drinking quite early in life, and I can barely remember a time when either was kind or nice. My grandmother adored my sister, and in the time they spent together, I suspect my sister observed quite a bit. It was from my grandmother, I believe, that my sister learned that those closest to addicts deserve little, should put up with anything, and should keep the peace at all costs. These points were all further driven home by my mother.

I, on the other hand, never spent any time with my grandparents, and because of that my early childhood was fairly protected and un-scathed.

My father was what you would call a functioning alcoholic, and he "functioned" until I was about ten years old. Somewhere around my tenth birthday, everything in my life began to change.

My parents started to fight; my father started to miss work and get into minor accidents, and the public humiliations began to increase. As my father's anger grew, he made scenes in public places, started arguments for no reason, and often left my mother stranded at events and parties because he wanted to go home and drink. Within two years, both my brothers and sister were gone to prep school, and I was left at home with parents who were in serious crisis. As things fell apart around us, they continued to tell me that everything was fine, nothing had changed, and we were the perfect family.

When friends brought my mother home from parties, she would say that my father was not feeling well and had wanted to leave early. If my father wrecked the car, she told me that someone else hit him. And if I asked about their fighting, my mother told me I must have been hearing things. My father simply said nothing.

I watched as my parents moved into separate bedrooms, quit speaking at dinner and barely went anywhere together. Lack of connection and communication became my parents' method of survival.

They withdrew from each other, they withdrew from their friends, and they withdrew from me. While my mother succeeded at keeping our home fairly anger free, it also became a home void of love or emotion.

With my parents as my role models, I learned to cope with the challenges of addiction. For the next 25 years, I would live basically cut off from any emotions, connections or real relationships with my family, my friends and my first husband. I basically went numb, using food and work to drown my anxiety and my feelings. I became so disconnected from myself that I did not even realize I had a problem.

In January of 2004, my oldest brother died of alcoholism. Three months later, my first husband passed away of the same disease. At that point, I began to worry that something was wrong with me, because I felt nothing. I remember clearly the day I went to see a therapist. She asked me why I had come. I told her that my grandfather, my father, my brother-in-law, my brother and my husband had all died of alcoholism and that I felt nothing — not loss, sadness, anger, nothing. It had become routine in my life that no matter how tragic, violent or scary the event, I handled it and moved forward as if everything was just fine. I told her that I thought that might not be normal.

That day started years of therapy to unravel what was a thick coat of armor of protection, denial and emotions buried so deep that they often exposed themselves in the most bizarre and inappropriate ways.

My journey back to a life of connection and communication is the reason I wanted to write this book and why I wanted it write it with my sister. The saddest part of our story is not the amount of addiction in our family. It is not the number of deaths. But rather it is our inability to talk about it, to be open about it, and to connect and relate to one another.

What I have learned is that tragedy strikes everyone, every family, and that addiction is a terrible thing, but that the real tragedy is when the family loses connection and does not communicate. To watch the energy and resources of the family all go into the addict, with nothing left for those impacted by the disease, is far sadder than the disease itself. Ours is a story of one addict — my grandfather — and ten en-ablers, who chose to give all of their energy, power and love to the addict until nothing was left for anyone else. The result was six more deaths from alcoholism, and four women who wasted years and big parts of their lives trying to save addicts, while losing themselves in the process.

This book is our journey; it is a journey out of addiction. It is a series of stories and lessons of how to **accept your life, gain knowledge and make good choices, so that you can create a positive and happy future**. It's about understanding that there is power in the choices you make, both positive and negative.

This book will help you make those choices wisely, and will ensure that you do not lose yourself, no matter what struggles you face. This book will show you how to stay engaged through authentic connec-tion and honest communication with everyone in your life and, most importantly, with yourself.

Introduction

Every time a news story on addiction ends with a well-meaning reporter saying, "Help is out there," or "Check with your doctor," or "Call this hotline," we want to scream. Maybe if you live in a major city, have an extra $20,000 a month for rehab and have a cooperative addict who wants help, then help is out there. But for the rest of us living with an active addict, we have only ourselves to depend on as we navigate through one impossible situation after another. Even if we have achieved "detachment," as Al-Anon wisely, wisely preaches, situations still arise that must be dealt with.

We (Meridith and Beth) have had to navigate life through six addictions thus far. Our grandfather. Our father. Our oldest brother. And both our first husbands. And during the writing of this book, our second brother, who was in the last stages of alcoholism, shot and killed himself. For the past two years he had been living with our mother, who was firmly ensconced in her role as enabler. This last scenario (elderly parent living with alcoholic child) presented us with all kinds of new challenges.

Needless to say, we have learned a lot along the way. We understand that you are most likely in an extremely uncomfortable place in your life right now or you wouldn't be reading this book. So we have filled these pages with practical advice, resources and real-life stories and experiences that are meant to help you better navigate these difficult times.

And while we are confident that you will find this book invaluable, we also know that it is and will always remain a guide and a resource, nothing more. We know from our own experience that you and you alone must reach and make the difficult decisions to change your life. And no matter how much advice and support you receive, in order for change to take hold, it must begin and end with you. Just like an addict is the only one who can decide to quit using, you are the only one who can decide when and how you will see the value in helping yourself.

So what we hope you find here is practical knowledge that helps to smooth your road. We hope that this book can help you no matter where you are on that road. Our goals for this book and for you are:

- We want you to know the signs of addiction, so you know where you and your addict are in the process, and what you can expect.

- We want you to know who can help — and maybe even more importantly, who can't — when you are ready to reach out.

- We want to give you some hard-learned tips on how best to keep yourself, your children and your family finances safe as the addiction progresses.

- Most of all, we want you to learn from our missteps, so you can get on with creating a life and living fully with or without your addict. We hope that this happens a lot faster for you — and with less heartache — than it did for us.

And if you are ready, we will also show you how to recognize signs of addictive behaviors in your own life and in the many so-called "normal" relationships you have. In general, society assigns addiction to activities such as drinking alcohol, drug use, shopping, gambling, eating, etc. In reality, that's a major misconception. As you read this book, you will see that addictive behaviors (manipulation, claiming victimhood, rescuing, guilt) are at work in many of our substance-free relationships. And if left unaddressed, the behaviors can have the same negative, long-term impact as they did in our relationships with more "traditional" addicts.

The information we put in this book — this survival guide, really — is the information we wish someone had handed us in our mid-teens, our early 20s and again in our mid-30s. It's information that, until now, you could only gain through experience. And while you may or may not be able to totally absorb the information and accept the hard facts at this moment, the practical advice, red flags and the permission to put yourself first are all here. So wherever you are now, keep this book close. When you are ready, the things you need to know will be ready too.

NOTE: We are just going to refer to addicts as "he" in this book because "he/she" seems awkward and "it" seems unkind. Unfortunately, the English language just hasn't come up with a gender-neutral singular pronoun yet.

Part One: You

Chapter 1:

Is He Really An Addict?

This is a question that all of us with addicts in our lives struggle with — especially in the beginning.

Addiction is confusing. Most of us don't see ourselves as experts in the field and able to diagnose this condition. And labeling a loved one an addict has serious consequences for our addict, for the whole family and for us. It only makes sense that we yearn for a formula, a calculation, a definitive answer.

When substance abuse is "the problem," "the problem" isn't black and white. You didn't just wake up one morning and find that, voila, your spouse, sibling, parent or child was a raging drug addict or alcoholic. The disease — and thus the behaviors that go with it — creeps into our lives, almost unnoticed at first. And then before we know it, behavior we would have once considered bizarre (both on our part and on the part of our addict) is now accepted, everyday behavior. At the same time, your addict is probably insisting that the behaviors you are complaining about are normal, that you are overreacting and that you don't know what you are talking about.

So let's make it easy. Let's change the question: **Do YOU have a problem?**

Since you are asking the question and reading this book, then something is most likely is bothering you. So the answer then is clearly "yes, you do have a problem."

The beauty of changing the question is that it doesn't matter if your loved one drinks a bottle of vodka every morning or has a few beers at the end of the day. You don't have to judge his actions. All you need to know is that whatever the behavior is, it bothers you. And that's where you need to be focused — on you. **Because you can control you. You cannot control your addict.**

Think about it this way: What if you could definitely identify your loved one as a bona-fide addict. What then? What would your next step be? How exactly would you go about changing the addict's behavior?

You are probably working your way through that futile list of actions now, much as we all have when in a relationship with an addict. And most likely, you are beginning to find that it's your behavior that is changing, not his, and that the problems are only mounting.

This is one of the most powerful lessons to learn in regard to addiction, so we want to repeat it. If you are changing your behavior in an effort to create some desired outcome in the addict, then this is the first sign that you have a problem.

Eventually, we come to live each day expecting the worst from our addicts and not much more. And eventually, they meet our expectations. We fill our days not with things that move us forward and make us feel good, but with planning preventative actions and neutralizing disasters to keep up the pretense of our lives.

We live our lives thinking that we are controlling the addict, when actually the addiction is controlling us.

If we really want to beat addiction, we need to take our worry, our nagging, our scheming, our praying and our energy off the addict, and put it toward something that we know we can change for the better — ourselves. This means that the best way to help your addict is to begin helping yourself. Take all the energy you were pouring into helping him and begin pouring into yourself.

Don't worry if you have no idea how to make this switch right now. As you move through this book, you will find step-by-step processes to help you shift your thinking to a successful strategy for dealing with addiction.

Bottom line: Don't look to an addict for answers. Trust yourself. Check in with yourself. What do you know for sure? (He drinks a six-pack every night and passes out on the couch. He involves alcohol in everything you do.) Is that a problem for YOU? (This is not living. I'm bored and anxious every night.) Your answers count. In fact, they are all that count.

Take Away:
You have a problem. You are the solution.

Chapter 2:

Enabling Is Not Helping—Here's Why

Helping your addict is hurting your addict — and yourself, for that matter.

Understanding, accepting and incorporating this concept into our own lives literally took years, maybe even decades — and we both still find ourselves tempted to enable from time to time.

When you think you are helping an addict — giving him money, food to eat or making excuses for him — you are not actually helping the person you love. Rather, you are giving his disease all the comforts it needs to thrive. This is called enabling.

By giving him a place to sleep or bailing him out of jail, you are in cahoots with the addiction and keeping the addict comfortably numb. You pay the bills, fix the car, call his boss — and he never feels the downside of addiction. You may see the reality of his life slipping away, but you are making sure he never gets the opportunity to feel it. And without the pain, there is nothing to alert his brain that he's in trouble.

But you say, he has no friends, no life, he's been arrested. Isn't that enough pain? Maybe for you that would be enough pain. However, your addict has become dulled to the pain thanks to his drug of choice. He passes those pain points on to you — the enabler — and you dutifully take the worst of the pain from him and fix what you can, so he can continue to imbibe. You put up the barriers so that he never reaches his pain threshold, and as a result, his addiction grows without challenge.

A case in point

As my (Meridith's) attractive, hard-working first husband began giving his life over to vodka, I — the dutiful wife and all around "good" person — began picking up whatever slack he dropped. As he slowly stopped earning his share of our life, I filled in whatever was needed. I paid the bills, sent the birthday cards, I even drove us everywhere, which allowed him to drink as much as he wanted without having to think about driving drunk. Worst of all, I went around insisting that we had a great marriage and that all was normal and healthy — though I'm sure that everyone who looked at his pale skin and slowly sinking face knew something was off.

Looking back now, all my efforts were creating a comfortable, all-expenses-paid space for his addiction to grow; a place where nothing was going to wake him from the fog of addiction. The more I did, the easier I made it for him to drink all day. Eventually, he stopped working. Stopped socializing. Stopped living.

Addicts abuse their drug of choice because they do not feel good about themselves. (The drugs and alcohol numb them from that feeling.) When we enable, we reinforce the addict's belief that they are not able, they are not good enough. Through our "doing for them," we tell them that we do not believe they can do it either.

During the last years of my husband's life, a therapist I knew gave me (Meridith) some wise advice. She told me that my husband had a core belief that he was not good enough, and that addicts in general abuse because they do not like — in fact, they even hate — themselves. The only way to heal this lack of self-love was to give him room to rebuild his self-confidence and self-worth. When I enabled him, I was actually destroying any chance of recovery. When I jumped in to "fix" his life, I was telling him — through my actions — that I did not believe that he was good enough to do it on his own.

The second time my husband entered recovery he was bound and determined to get his life together. His body was weak from withdrawal, so he decided to join a gym to get his strength back. I was so excited. This was a good sign. I knew he had not been working, so I quickly ran down and paid his gym membership for three months. Then I began asking him things like, "Do you want to work out together?" or "What time are you going to the gym today?" Within three weeks he had quit going to the gym. There is no proof that my enabling did that. But the truth is I never gave him the encouragement or support; I never showed him that I believed he could stand on his own two feet. My enabling smothered his spark for recovery.

My therapist helped me see what I had done by using my own life as an example. She asked me to think about times in my life when I had overcome obstacles, challenges and fear. She asked me to question if I gained more confidence and self-worth from doing things myself or when others did for me. Again, strong and wise words that I wish I had learned far earlier in our relationship.

It would be wonderful if there were a pill that could stop an addict from using and change his behavior. But there is not. (Though there are some medicines out there that supposedly help; that has not been our direct experience.) All we have right now is the slim chance that the addict will feel the pain of his disease and, from that, find the will to stop. Our enabling fuels the addiction and destroys even that slim chance. For now, **the only person who can help an addict is an addict.**

Take away:
Your enabling behaviors encourage the addiction.

Chapter 3:

Detachment Is Love

There is a cure for enabling. It's called detachment. And while it may sound like a cold solution to those standing outside addiction, it is the warmest act of love you can give to another human being, especially someone suffering with addiction.

People suffering with an addiction deserve compassion, not anger. Their inexplicable, self-destructive actions tell us that **addiction is an illness, not a simple choice**. Someone who is merely selfish or cruel would not drink themselves into jail or intensive care.

When you practice detachment, it gives your addict the opportunity to receive the pain signals and the inner confidence to move toward recovery. It also helps diffuse your anger by putting you back in control of your life. Will it be the life you planned? No. But then, that's life. **Detachment is not rejecting the person you love; rather it is starving the addiction.** By creating compassionate boundaries between yourself and the addiction, you are saying to your addict, "I love you. I want you to live. I will do everything in my power to support your sobriety and that means not supporting your addiction."

Knowing where to draw these "compassionate boundaries," however, is where detachment gets tricky for us enablers. This is hard stuff.

Just as our addicts won't be perfect in their recovery, we enablers won't be perfect in our detachment. So be compassionate with yourself as well. Our experience with detachment is one step forward, one freak out and then two steps back.

Much like addiction, enabling (our disease) creeps into our lives as well. What begins as seemingly reasonable acts of kindness toward a loved one slowly becomes a constant and exhausting juggling act to keep our addicts out of trouble, our households running and ourselves sane — all of which, despite our best efforts, continue to spin out of control.

A case in point

Just after my first husband and I (Beth) were married, he started complaining of throat pain. Well, when someone says they are sick, you encourage them to go to the doctor, right? A reasonable act of kindness. So that's what I did.

The doctor was unable to determine exactly what was wrong but gave my husband pills for the pain. Though we had health insurance, we still had to pay deductibles and pay for the "medicine." We were not wealthy and this was an expense for us — but it was medicine that was "prescribed by a doctor," so we found the money and paid for it.

As the years went on, my husband's un-diagnosable ailments spread to his back and to an elbow. Eventually, he came down with the king of all un-diagnosable ailments, the headache. (At the time, I was too naive to know that addicts often present with un-diagnosable ailments to get a steady supply of drugs from doctors.) All his pains led to more medical appointments, several hospital visits for tests, loads of painkillers and mounting bills.

Thus, what started as a normal act on my part — encouraging someone who says he feels sick to see a doctor — grew into a circus of ailments, doctors, painkillers and unpaid bills. And as for my part in it, I never questioned it or said enough is enough, though it was making me increasingly unhappy and broke. I saw myself as selfish for being angry and not believing he was "sick."

In fact, being the good enabler that I was, I was exhausting myself organizing and paying the bills. A non-enabler might ask why I felt it was my responsibility to organize and pay the bills. But my thinking was that since my husband wouldn't do it, I had to do it to keep us out of debt and keep up appearances. (Later, you'll get some strategies on how to make decisions when your thinking gets blurry like that.)

The results of my enabling were about the same as Sisyphus rolling that boulder up a hill just to watch it roll back down, cursed to repeat the futile act for eternity. Our debts obviously weren't going away. The more I paid out, the more he could go to the doctor, the more pain pills he could get, the less he worked, the more bills came in, the more I paid, and so on and so on.

In the end, it was my enabling, not his addiction, that kept my husband and me blind to the reality of our lives. Who was I helping? The answer is no one. My enabling was hurting everyone.

Putting Sisyphus's rock to rest begins with detachment.

Detaching

The first step to detaching is becoming aware of our actions. The second step is owning them. No more saying, "I had to because..." Whether you are paying a delinquent bill or giving him a ride because he has lost his license, you need to realize that you, the enabler, "did" so because you "chose" to. Ouch.

Before you do anything or pay for anything that involves your addict:

11

- Check in with yourself and ask why you are doing it. *Are you really helping him? Or are you avoiding confrontation or trying to save face for yourself?*
- What will it accomplish? *If I pay his car insurance now, what will that accomplish? He will be able to drink and drive his car for another month. So I'll get to worry about that for another 30 days. And next month, I'll have another bill to pay or worse.*
- What is your real goal and will this action move you closer to it? *If your goal is to help your addict recover, is your paying his car insurance moving him any closer to realizing his condition, getting a job or going to a detox center? Or is your action making his addiction more comfortable for him?*
- Take responsibility for that answer and whatever action you choose to take. *Sometimes you will choose to enable. Heck, I (Beth) bought my husband a new refrigerator after I left the home, just to avoid confrontation. I didn't want to listen to another round of how I wasn't living up to my wedding vows. Ridiculous now, I know, but addicts know how to push our buttons. It was just easier — though not really good for him or my bank account — to enable in that moment. However, I knew that's what I was doing and didn't complain about it to him later. Just realize that the choice is yours. No one made it for you.*

After a lifetime of enabling, detachment is a hard concept to put into practice. It's hard sometimes to know which actions cross the line into enabling. Many of us were raised by enablers to be enablers.

Our mother and father were both champion enablers — sacrificing everyone and everything they loved to indulge the addicts in their lives. It's the only behavior we really know. Our natural default is to take the self-denying, controlling, enabling action — to handle it ourselves — and then be angry with the addict for making us do it.

Our father moved himself and his new bride (our mother) from the promise of an exciting career and lively social life in White Plains, New York, to a small, depressing coal town outside of Pittsburgh, where he took over his father's insurance agency. He made this move at the request of his mother, who cried to him that she could no longer tolerate his alcoholic father and that he, her son, would have to move home to deal with the situation.

Despite our mother's protestations and her offer to have his mother come live with them in New York, my father chose to enable his mother. We ended up living one street over from them. As a result, our mother always carried some resentment toward our father because she hated the town and loathed my father's father. (The feeling was mutual.) Our father was angry because he was a bright man who had given up a career he loved in a place he loved to run a small insurance agency in a town where good conversations were few and far between. We children, especially our brothers, were exposed to our grandfather's crazy behavior and grew up in a place where we didn't fit in. And the rest, as they say, is history. As you know, depression plagued our father and both our brothers; all eventually drank themselves to death.

Think of the difference it would have made in everyone's life if our father had practiced detachment and drawn compassionate boundaries around the situation. What if he had told his mother that he was not coming back but that his door was open to her. And what if our grandmother had detached and chosen to leave her alcoholic husband and walk through that open door. What if our mother, the new bride, had put her foot down right then and there and said she would not go to southwestern Pennsylvania.

As you can see, it would have taken immense strength and self-awareness for any of these people to make different choices. Society teaches us to go down with the ship, even if everyone else on the ship is already drowning.

If you have the insight and courage, detachment can get you and all the other people in your life off the addict's sinking ship. It also puts the addict one step closer to shore.

The best place we have found to come to a practical understanding of detachment is Al-Anon. Al-Anon meetings are plentiful and free. (You can find a meeting near you at www.al-anon.org.) You don't have to say anything. You don't even have to introduce yourself. Just go and listen to people at the meetings, until one day you say "aha!" because you finally understand the true cruelty of enabling and the love that is found in detachment.

Addicts have to try a few AA or NA meetings before the message sinks in, so don't be surprised if the first time you try Al-Anon you leave with the feeling that you will never go back. Remain open, listen to the message and always be willing to give it another try. Both of us had to give Al-Anon four to six tries before the message took hold and the lessons began to make sense. So go without judgment. If it helps, go back. If it does not, just remain open to returning when you feel the need.

Al-Anon's lessons are powerful and so life affirming that everyone — whether dealing with an addict or not — would be fortunate to integrate them into daily life. But the messages are different from what our society espouses and may seem illogical or uncomfortable at first. Like all change, it takes time.

By the way, if you do choose to attend an Al-Anon meeting and your addict knows it, he will accuse you of going there to bad-mouth him. Addicts, as we're sure you have noticed, think everything is about them. Your Al-Anon meeting, however, will be all about you.

Be warned

As you become more aware of your actions, begin to draw compassionate boundaries and stop enabling, people are going to judge you.

Some of these judgments will be harsh. Folks who used to say you were an angel are now going to say, "How could you let him…."

From the outside, our compassionate boundaries may seem cruel, but they are far from it. Do not listen to anyone who has not lived with addiction. They have no idea what you are up against and how irrational addiction is. Taking feedback from them would be like taking parenting advice from someone who has never lived through a two-year-old's tantrum. They can have all the theories in the world, but unless they've been in the trenches, they simply do not know.

To bolster your resolve to stay true to the boundaries you've made, remember that your actions have an impact on others in your life beyond the addict. When you make a choice to enable an addict, you are often making a choice to hurt someone else. Your children, your friends and your family are learning from you.

Be prepared for people close to you and the addict himself to tell you that you are heartless. Many of these people are invested in you keeping the addict under control so that they don't have to deal with him. When you begin to draw boundaries and expose the truth of addiction, you upset their world. Again, this includes parents, friends, in-laws and even healthcare professionals — but more about that later.

Your addict is definitely going to tell you that you are heartless and clueless, and that you don't understand. But he has neither his best interest nor your best interest at heart. **The only entity with a survival instinct here is the addiction itself.**

Identify the real foe

If your addict is an adult, remember that you are not talking to an adult. Realize that you are talking to a disease. Trying to reason with an addict is a waste of energy — and they can usually talk circles around you anyway.

Know that your addict's behavior is in no way a reflection on the relationship you had with him. That's because, as we've said, there is no "him" anymore. His goal every day is to numb himself so that he cannot feel. And you can't have a relationship with someone who can't feel. The relationship you are in now is really between his addiction and your enabling. He has to drink because you are a nag. You have to nag because you are "right." The only way out of this circle is for either the addict or the enabler to stop participating.

Know that his rage at you is really rage at himself. You can stay active with this rage and let him place all the blame on you. Or you detach and put him one person closer to having only himself to deal with.

I (Meridith) believe two of the lessons I am most grateful for (and the lessons I would most want someone to learn, whether they have an addict in their life or not, are those of detachment and compassionate boundaries. These are powerful lessons that take time to learn but will change your life. The day I woke up and realized that I needed help, that I was truly as sick as my addict, was the day I took my first step toward detachment. And with that detachment came compassion.

That day, I realized that my addict, in this moment in time, was not going to change no matter how much I wanted him to. No matter how much I yelled, screamed, helped, begged, or pleaded — or loved him — he was still going to abuse. I also realized that he was an adult and that he was free to choose how he wanted to live or not live. I was also an adult, and I had those same choices. I realized that as much as I wanted him to quit abusing, he wanted me to quit begging him to stop abusing.

This made us two people who loved one another but who wanted very different lives. He wanted to be an addict married to a woman who allowed him to be active in his alcohol abuse. I wanted to be married to an addict who was actively working to quit. Neither one of us, in this moment, was willing to give up what we wanted.

With that realization, my detachment began. The understanding that he wanted me to change as much as I wanted him to change brought home how much I could not change him. I knew there was no way he could ever convince me to change. Putting it in that perspective made me realize that I could not change him any more than he could change me.

What followed was compassion. From that day forward, every day that I spoke or wrote to him, I told him that I loved him, cared about him, wished he would get help, and that if he ever committed to getting sober (meaning that he found the rehab himself and checked himself in) that I would be there for him. Until then, I could not be a part of his life or have him be part of mine.

Why am I grateful for this lesson? Although my addict never recovered, I am so grateful my very last words to him were those. The last letter I wrote him closed with those words and the last conversation we had ended the same. And for the last year of his life, we never had a cross word between us. He knew he was loved, knew help was there if he wanted it and knew that the door was open if he ever chose to walk through it.

Detachment and compassionate boundaries freed me from guilt and anger, and provided a small silver lining of love between two people in an incredibly sad and tragic situation. I will forever be grateful that in the last year of my husband's life—unlike those during our marriage — he received from me compassion and kindness instead of anger and rage.

Now, I understand that the outcome — his death — might seem unacceptable to you where your own addict is concerned. And really, it is still unacceptable to me. But take the time to think about what my alternative was. My fighting his addiction every day was fueling his addiction and taking us both down in the process. With detachment and compassion, I stopped being an active partner with his addiction. It allowed us both to take the focus off our relationship and put it where it needed to be — on the disease. Through detachment, a positive space was created, a space where if he was able to find the strength to choose recovery, I would be there for him.

The power of powerlessness

When writing this book, we were given advice to find a story to reflect detachment that had a happier ending. The point being that it would give you, our reader, hope that if you detached, your addict might get sober. We could have done that. After all, some addicts do recover. But we realized that would have defeated the true purpose of learning to detach—which is to surrender. Just as addicts need to accept that they are powerless against their drug of choice, we enablers need to accept that we are powerless to save the addict. We are not God (we know that's hard for enablers to hear). We don't get to control the outcome of someone else's life.

The purpose of learning to detach is just that, detachment. Our choice not to put a story here with the proverbial happy ending is to help you understand that detachment is not a way to save your addict. It is a way to continue to actively love your addict and let him feel that love. Detachment allows you to stop your personal rage and anger, and to accept the person.

As you learned earlier in this book, only the addict can help the addict. You can provide love, you can provide support if and when they want to recover, but the choice to recover remains theirs. Without learning to detach, you will often drive the addict away or worse. Your anger, judgment and rage just feed the addiction.

Again, no matter if your addict recovers or continues to suffer, learning to detach shows your loved one that you believe in him to do the hard work of recovery and tells him that should he choose to recover, he has someone to turn to.

I (Meridith) continue to actively use detachment in my life. Years ago, a friend's "social drinking" reached the point where his behavior was uncomfortable for me. After three DUI's and being forced to blow into a breathalyzer every time he drove a car, he still felt he did not have a problem. Though the fact was his daily consumption of alcohol was visibly increasing.

While his drinking was not a problem for him, it had become a problem for me. Due to his actions, I no longer trusted him, enjoyed his company or felt confident in his ability to handle business for me. Though he continued to reassure me that things were under control, for me, it was time to detach. During one of our regular meetings and once he completed his update on our project, I decided to share my feelings and to detach.

I began by saying that I felt his drinking had become a problem for me and that I thought he needed help. (He immediately became defensive, angry and upset. I just asked for permission to continue.) I shared that I respected his right to live his life however he wanted and I hoped he would respect my right to do the same.

I let him know that his drinking and his actions had reached a point where I no longer felt comfortable in his ability to make business decisions on my behalf. In addition, I let him know that his drinking made me feel unsafe, anxious and uncomfortable when I was around him. And for now, until he was ready get help, I could no longer have him actively in my life either professionally or personally. While I cared about him both as a friend and as a business advisor, until he was open to getting help and dealing with what I felt was an issue, I could no longer be involved with him. I ended by again, letting him know that I cared for him and was worried about him, and that if he ever wanted to get help, I would be there for him.

Detachment is not easy in the moment, but it frees you. It allows you to be in a position to truly help your friends and family if and when they ever need you. It also, prevents you from going down the path of resentment, anger and guilt.

Take Away:
The more you enable, the further from recovery you push your addict. Draw and adhere to compassionate boundaries.

Chapter 4:

Yes, But ...

At this point, you may be thinking that your situation is really different from ours and those of all the other alcoholics, addicts and enablers we've met along this road. You may be thinking that your loved one does have a problem, YES, BUT ... really, it's nothing like what we are describing in this book. It's not that desperate. He's not displaying all those behaviors. Just a few ring true. Right now, you just can't see how your life could ever get as bad as ours did.

We get that. In truth, you and the person you love who has an addiction are unique individuals. However, the disease and the enabling that goes along with it are not. You are now on a well-worn path, whether you choose to recognize it or not. And if you are finding yourself saying, "YES, BUT...," then you are at a point on that path where we and a million others have been as well.

Meridith

When my first husband, Doug, and I sought the advice of a therapist for "marriage" issues, she asked me at one point, "Do you still love him?"

I answered truthfully. "Yes."

She then turned to him and said, "You are an addict. Right now, she still loves you and wants to be married to you. But if you don't stop drinking, there will come a day, not too long from now, where she will reach her edge, she will have had enough, and there will be nothing you can do to save your marriage. If you don't admit you have a problem, if you don't quit drinking, alcohol will take your marriage and ultimately take your life."

I didn't believe her. I couldn't imagine ever leaving him; our marriage was hurting, YES, BUT there would never come a day when I would leave him. YES, my husband had problems, BUT he wasn't an addict. YES, his drinking was a big enough issue to send us to counseling, BUT he wasn't in that kind of trouble. I had a picture in my mind of what an addict was, and my husband wasn't that.

I also had rules about what constituted an alcoholic, and he didn't fit them. He never drank at lunch, and he didn't drink before 4 p.m. We had even talked to each other about people we thought had drinking problems because they drank at noon.

He came from a stable family — his parents had been happily married for 30 years and were great people. We both had careers. We had loads of friends. We owned a home. We were fun people. In my mind, these were not things an alcoholic could do or be. Therefore, I reasoned, what the therapist said could not be true. He wasn't an addict.

What actually was true at that point was that I was using the outside facts of our lives to cover the truth of the inside. It's like being bankrupt, but still — for the moment — sitting in your house with your jewelry on and a car in the driveway. From the outside, life still looks good, but the things you need to sustain that fiction are fading away.

Inside our lives, his drinking had driven us to seek counseling. Inside, he was beginning to withdraw from the world. Inside, we really weren't having that much fun. He was having difficulty at work — always someone else's fault, of course. We were not communicating. He no longer accompanied me to events I had for my work. And our lives were beginning to diverge. We no longer had common goals.

Within a few years, everything that therapist said would happen did happen. I did leave my husband. And he did die from alcoholism. In fact, this smart, funny man with a loving family and scores of friends who truly cared for him died alone in a hotel room.

Alcoholics come in all shapes and sizes, from all walks of life and with all different types of experiences. You may think that your own addict is different, but the sad truth is that no matter how you disguise it to yourself, he is not.

Beth

I (Beth) remember the first time my husband and I looked into a residential treatment center for his addiction. The woman running the center said to him, "To recover from addiction, you have to be willing to do anything. If I tell you to get on your knees and push a super ball with your nose down this hallway naked to achieve recovery, you will jump at the offer."

I thought to myself, YES he needs some help, BUT does he really need to be humiliated? He's not some low-life person with no pride. What I didn't understand is that she wasn't talking about humiliation. She was talking about surrender. And what she knew — that I had yet to admit — is that he didn't have any pride when it came to drugs. He would have rolled a ball down Main Street naked for drugs. He needed that same commitment to be successful in recovery.

Within a year of that meeting and an unsuccessful rehab, the results of his addiction had stripped the charade of pride from both of us. At that time, if someone had told me that all I had to do to end this nightmare was push a ball down Main Street with my nose, while naked, I would have jumped at the chance.

Our mother

And finally, just a few years ago, our mother sat in a therapist's office. The therapist told her straight to her face that her son, Ted, was an alcoholic and that if she kept supporting him he would die. After losing a husband, a son and two sons-in-law to addiction, she said to the therapist, "YES, BUT...." Ted was different. Ted had self-respect. Ted was smart. Ted was good looking. Ted had a good job. She could help Ted get back on his feet. So against the advice of the therapist, against the pleas of her daughters, she took him into her home. And by now you know the rest of that story.

You

Recovery, like addiction, begins with a whisper. Yet, as you can see from our experiences, even when someone shouted the truth directly at us, we couldn't hear past all the denial in our heads—and we're the sober ones. So, as you read on, if you find yourself saying, "YES, BUT," just be aware of it. Stop the talk in your head for a moment, take a deep breath and open yourself to listening. It could save both you and your addict a lot of pain.

The difficult part of recognizing addiction is that it can look different in the beginning. But no matter how the situation appears at first, understand that without help and support it will get worse. Just when you think your addict has hit bottom, he will go further, and his bottom is beyond your imagination.

My (Meridith's) husband was handsome, talented and smart. He took pride in the work that he did and was dedicated to doing it right and ahead of schedule. The first time he missed a deadline, it bothered me, but I dismissed it and believed his story that the materials had not come in time. As he missed more and more deadlines and lost a job here and there, I continued to ignore it and still tell myself that he was OK. As the work slowed down, the television watching increased and the friends disappeared, I continued to remain in denial. Then one day our neighbor's son, who was home from medical school, called me at work in a panic. He had found my handsome, smart husband buck naked, passed out in our backyard at 3 in the afternoon. He was drunk. Our neighbor was scared and had called an ambulance. He was worried that my husband might die. He asked how long he had been having these problems.

Even my young neighbor knew I was married to an addict. It was time for me to wake up and realize that "YES, BUT" no matter how this had started, no matter who my husband had been before the addiction, the disease itself was headed down a familiar, identifiable path. The end point was a known outcome. We had a problem.

Take Away:
When someone speaks a hard truth, listen.

Chapter 5:

Find Your Inner Compass and Head in That Direction

Remember the old adage, **"Actions speak louder than words."** Make that your mantra.

Addicts lie. They lie unbelievably well and lie constantly, about things you would never expect. They lie about things when they have no reason to lie. We may think that we are dealing with the sweet child we raised, the loving person we married, or the parent who was always there for us. But once substance abuse seeps into their lives, we must realize that whoever our addict was before is gone. GONE. The addiction is talking now. And whatever our addict says — even to himself — is probably a lie.

Though from time to time you may glimpse the person you knew, you can no longer trust anything he says.

(NOTE: If you are just starting this journey, we know you may not yet be able to accept this fully. That's OK. Just keep this tidbit of information in mind for now; you're going to need it to give you clarity and acceptance later. If you feel confused, put the guideline "actions speak louder than words" into play, and it will help you sort your situation out.)

As addiction takes an addict's brain, it takes their character as well. They will say or do anything to keep abusing; this is not hyperbole. In the beginning, you will see it as little lies, such as slightly under reporting how much they got paid (so they can hide how much they are spending on alcohol or drugs). As the disease progresses, so do the significance and consequences of the lies.

You should also be aware that someone who is actively enabling an addict also is prone to lying. For instance, if you have one parent who is an addict and the other parent has been enabling for 40 years, chances are you won't get a straight answer from either of them. Both are heavily invested in their roles in the addiction. We don't need to judge this. As enablers, we are all guilty of refusing to see the truth and lying to protect our illusions. As we emerge from our fog of enabling, we just need to be aware of it in others to keep our own decision-making abilities straight.

Needless to say, dealing with a liar is extremely difficult on both emotional and practical levels. It makes you feel crazy, because you are not sure what's what. But you are not crazy. You are simply not getting the information you need to make good decisions and manage your life. So here is how to get uncrazy.

Here's what you do when you make a decision

1. Remain cautious of your addict's (or active enabler's) words. Let him say it. No need to argue. But don't use information you've been given by an addict, even if it seems to make sense.
2. Decide what you know for sure about the situation. The facts. Past behavior, etc.
3. If you feel a need to be involved, get outside confirmation on things you are not sure of (i.e., call the school and make sure that they really don't have class on Monday). Again, there is

no need to confront the addict. But having correct information will calm you down and help you to make better decisions for yourself.

4. Make your decision based on what you know for sure, not what your addict says. Trust you and only you, no matter how much they argue. (This is huge for most enablers, but you get used to it.)

5. Learn to separate words from actions. Make your decisions based on what your addict does, the action he does or does not take, rather than the words he says.

This last step is especially crucial. And when you learn to do it — to separate words from actions — you will find it invaluable in dealing with an addict and in dealing with many people in life.

Here's an example of how to make a decision. Our mother finally got our alcoholic brother Ted to agree to donate one of his two wrecked cars (sitting illegally in her driveway) to charity. He then told her that he had called the charity and that they said they needed him to fix the transmission before they would take it. So she would need to give him $1,000 so he could have that fixed.

OK. What do we know?

- We know that our brother is an alcoholic. So we do not take his word as truth. We know that the charity says on its website that they'll pick up any car, as long as it has an engine.
- We know that the car does in fact have an engine.
- We know the phone number of the charity, so if we want to, we can call to ask if the car has to have a transmission.
- We know that if they won't take the car, then we can certainly find a salvage place that will take it for free.
- Most important, we know that we don't give an alcoholic $1,000 — no matter what the situation.

For the purposes of this book, we did e-mail the nonprofit, and they wrote back saying that the only requirement was that the tires and wheels of the car move freely so that the tow truck could pick it up.

This brings us to another little saying that helped us stay grounded and keep from falling victim to an addict's reasoning: "If it sounds crazy, it is crazy." Why would you spend $1,000 on a transmission for a car you are going to donate to charity? That's crazy.

(By the way, our brother never donated the car to charity or sold it like he told our mother he would. The car remained in her driveway, and she continued to receive angry letters from the homeowners association. Removing the car got placed on our — Meridith and Beth's — to-do list after his death.)

Post-rehab lying

The most dangerous time for you to fall victim to an addict's lying is right after he returns from rehab. You have glimpsed your addict sober for a few weeks; the person you know and love is back. You have so much emotionally invested in his recovery. Your heart and mind want desperately to believe that he has returned and that everything will be OK.

However, the majority of addicts who go through rehab relapse. Most addicts experience recovery as a one-step-forward, two-steps-back process. Even an addict who is committed to regaining his life goes through this process. To keep yourself sane, to protect those around you, and to keep your addict accountable — which is what he needs to have his best chance for recovery — you need to continue to live by your mantra of "actions speak louder than words."

In fact, if he begins to attack you for being cautious, you can bet that something is up. If you hear words like "you don't trust me," "you're not supportive of my sobriety," etc., it probably means that he is already using. You don't need to judge his words, though. You need to focus on the addict's actions, do what you know is best and trust your gut.

If it feels wrong to you, trust that and learn to believe in yourself and your instincts.

If you find that you are falsely accusing your recovering addict, don't beat yourself up. Part of the recovery is for the recovering addict to earn your trust back if he wants it. It's on his shoulders. Not yours.

I (Meridith) accused my first husband of drinking when he returned from rehab. He used my false accusations to make me feel guilty. And I did feel guilty. But now when I look back on it, I see that I had every right to be suspicious and express those suspicions. Part of his recovery and mine was to recognize and accept that lack of trust and do what was necessary to rebuild it. Obviously, we didn't understand that and we didn't get there.

The rock and the hard place

Even after we look at actions not words, successfully detach and base our decisions on what actually is, we may still find ourselves between a rock and a hard place from time to time. When you are related to an addict, situations continue to arise that call for impossible choices. However, having boundaries creates the space to see the situation clearly, weigh options and make the best possible choice.

A friend of ours has a son in his 20s who has been battling addiction since high school. As tough as it was to do, our friend has drawn compassionate boundaries with her son that have given him room to work toward recovery. This has also allowed her and the rest of the family to function. His road to recovery has been hard; some successes, many setbacks, but at least now he knows that it is **HIS** road.

Recently, though, our friend has been faced with a situation that would make Solomon weep in frustration. Her son and his girlfriend had a baby. This infant lives with the girlfriend, who has custody and who our friend suspects is an active addict.

Our friend, of course, is worried about her grandchild. She suspects that the baby's mother uses drugs in front of the child but has

31

no proof. And from her experience with other addicts in her life, our friend knows that she is only witnessing a very small percentage of what really goes on in the household.

So what does a responsible grandparent do in this situation? A grandparent who knows the value of detaching and keeping boundaries? A grandparent who has no rights to the baby and could be cut off completely as a lifeline for the infant if she angers either parent?

We don't have an answer to this, because obviously there is no glaring "right" answer. But when we find ourselves in such places, we do have a strategy that has helped us decide what to do or not do. We remove ourselves emotionally from the situation (if that is even possible in such a situation) — get rid of the pre-addiction backstory. We do not look at who the addict was before or who he could be, but rather, we look at the situation as it is right now. We pretend that we are strangers looking in on people we don't know.

For example, if we looked unemotionally at our friend's situation, we would see an infant being cared for by a parent who is using drugs to the point that she is not functioning as an adult (no job, no visible means of support). That's not a safe environment for a child. A rational person would get the baby out of that situation.

Our answer to our friend was, of course, that she needed to do whatever she felt comfortable doing and whatever she had the strength to do and to live with. We hoped that if we were ever in her situation, we'd have the strength to call social services and report the situation. Of course, that phone call brings more rocks and more hard places: Do you let the baby go into the foster care system? Or do you take your grandchild and involve yourself and other family members in a very emotional, no-win situation with the addict? What if social services doesn't do anything? And on and on. No easy answers.

Our friend adds to this and wisely warns that as enablers we must be careful that we don't get involved and invested in actions where we are trying to "force a solution." For instance, calling the police to say your addict is in possession of cocaine. "Forcing solutions" takes us right back down the rabbit hole codependency—with all the drama and expectations that come with it.

In the end, she felt calling social services for her was "forcing a solution." However, our friend did take some action she was comfortable with that ultimately resulted in some protection for her grandchild. She discussed her concerns openly with her son. As she puts it, she "spoke her truth" without expectation. After hearing her truth, he consulted a private attorney, who was a family relation, to explore options. Our friend did not get involved, though she supported her son emotionally. Her son and the attorney had the court look into the girlfriend's fitness as a parent. It was determined that the girlfriend had taken drugs recently. So now the court system is monitoring the girlfriend, and the baby has a court-appointed guardian. Though not a perfect solution, our friend is more at ease knowing a source outside the family is aware of and watching over her grandchild. Best of all, it is a source the addict cannot manipulate or threaten.

When our mother moved our alcoholic brother Ted to her home in our town several years ago, we were faced with a rock-and-hard-place decision. Do we let this desperate man move in with our enabling mother, steal from her and maybe even hurt her?

After alternating between hyperventilating and declaring ultimatums, we eventually used our strategy and removed ourselves from the situation to take an objective look. Our conclusion was that our mother was an adult. This was her house, her life and her money. We could run around waving our arms in the air, but in the end, we could not stop her. So we didn't.

We did express our opinion, and we sat down with her and shared our thoughts, our fears and our feelings on the situation. Then we drew our own boundary. We let her know that as long as she had an active alcoholic living with her, we would not be visiting her in her house. Her active alcoholic would not be invited to our homes either. We also chose not to ask her to put her valuables in storage or monitor her bank accounts.

As the months progressed into years, we worked hard to stay separate from the day-to-day catastrophes of her living with an alcoholic. And yes, neighbors and friends were asking where we were and why we weren't helping our mother, among other things. Our mother herself was pretty angry with us. She thought that we were cruel for not including Ted at the holidays and other social events.

We were not always successful at not enabling her during this time. We did get involved on occasion, such as when we met her at the hospital and took care of the paperwork and details while Ted was in the intensive care unit. But we remained aware of our actions. When we did enable her, we recognized it for what it was and recognized that we chose to do it.

So even though we drew our boundary, we were and still are affected by and dealing with the fall out of an addiction. We put our mother's house back in order after Ted died. We are handling his bill collectors. And we are doing our best to help our mother recover and regain a good life, ever conscious of our tendencies to enable.

No matter what you do or how well you draw your boundaries, the rocks and the hard places are going to show up. But detaching and dealing with the best truth you can uncover can allow you to handle the impossible situations better and without anger.

Remember that you are an adult. You are the sober one. You are in charge of your life. You make the decisions independently of any information you get from the addict or the enabler. Don't let anyone convince you othe

---

Take Away:
Actions speak louder than words.

Chapter 6:

The Scary Truth

In the beginning of Chapter 2, we asked why the addict doesn't stop — doesn't he feel enough pain? The time has come to turn that question on ourselves. Why don't we stop enabling? Isn't lying to our close friends, family, employers and co-workers, being lied to by the very person we love, ruining ourselves financially and never knowing what we will find when we come home painful enough?

Obviously not. We both continued to support our lies for years, costing ourselves unbearable stress and loads of money, all while not improving our addicts' health one little bit. So much waste.

Just like the addict finds it more comfortable and less painful to abuse his substance of choice than to get clean, we, the enablers, find it more comfortable and less painful to keep covering the truth with our deeds.

I (Beth) did not leave my husband because I told myself that I couldn't bear to take my son from his father and break up the family. I had taken a vow so I had to stay. (A behavior, by the way, I saw patterned by my mother.) The truth though was a far different story. What family? What father? I slept every night with my body in a circle around my baby to protect him from an extremely high, out-of-control addict. Not a father. Why would a caring mother even let her child near someone in that condition?

It's the magical thinking of the enabler. I was pretending that the interesting, fun-loving man I had married was still present. I was so invested in the life I had planned that I was going to force everyone — including my innocent child — to go along with it, even though it no longer existed. My husband's life was clearly on another path. As enablers, we spend our lives hoping for what we had planned rather than accepting what is.

It took a lot more pain, many more scary moments, a huge amount of money and much disappointment before I finally began to realize that his behavior was beyond my control and that the constant monitoring was taking an extreme toll on my ability to function. After three or four attempts, I finally left my husband for good, telling myself as I went out the door that should he improve, we could always remarry.

By that time, I was so mentally beaten down and so unable to believe in myself that I literally had trouble picking out what to wear each day. My head was so filled with his lies and my desperate need to believe them that I second-guessed myself on everything.

But with the Great Smoky Mountains between us (I moved from Tennessee to North Carolina), the fog of lies slowly dissipated, and I started to see and deal with the truth of what addiction and enabling had made of our lives. Step by tiny step, I stopped enabling him. And I realized that raising my son in a secure environment, with people and situations he could trust, was more important than having a pretend intact family. (More on this later.)

Just as the addict drags down those around him, so does the out-of-control enabler. You are living a lie when you cover his tracks at every turn — a lie in which you are willing to involve everyone you come in contact with.

We are not the victims here. The scary truth is that, as enablers, we have no one to blame but ourselves for where we are and how we are living. We choose to stay, to enable, to keep our addicts comfortable in their addiction. Now that stings! But it is also empowering. Once we realize that we don't have to keep reacting to the addict but are in control of our own actions, we can make smart choices that benefit everyone, including ourselves.

When I (Meridith) first started claiming my culpability in my first husband's addiction, I asked, "Why do I do this to myself?" But the answer to that question is multi-layered and could take years of therapy to unravel. Now, when I see my enabling tendencies appear, I ask, **"Why do I choose to be unhealthy today?"** The answer is usually resistance to the truth of the situation. So I take a deep breath and try my best to figure out the truth and then the answer and thus the healthiest action. I continue to use this question today, whenever I find myself in an uncomfortable situation.

Take Away:
If you want to stop your dance with addiction, you, the enabler, must leave the floor. We are not victims. We are responsible for our choices.

Part Two: Your Addict

Chapter 7:

Behaviors You Can Count On

If you have any doubt that addiction is a disease, you only have to look at your loved one to know that it's true. As the disease progresses, it takes a physical toll. The skin loses color and elasticity, the eyes dull and capillaries throughout the face break causing redness and a possible cauliflower nose. Hair becomes brittle, muscles wither. Teeth rot due to lack of saliva. The chest sinks in and the stomach bloats. You might also notice a yellowing in the eyes due to jaundice, which indicates poor liver function. In addition, the addict finds it difficult to sleep through the night and eventually stops eating. Add the constant shaking, and by the end, the addict looks like someone suffering from a terminal illness. Because he is suffering from a terminal illness.

As you know, this disease affects the mind as well as the body. So along with the physical changes, you begin to witness behavioral changes. In the beginning, many of the behaviors of the addicted personality seem innocent enough (e.g., complaining about a mean boss or a backache). So as a novice enabler you might have normal reactions to these events (condemning the boss, encouraging a visit to the doctor).

But these events, like other predictable, addictive behaviors, are just a means to an end with an addict. The more aware you are of the behaviors that accompany addiction, the more prepared you will be to recognize them right away for what they truly are.

One thing to keep in mind is that whatever behaviors you see, you can be sure that they are only the tip of the iceberg. Traffic tickets, wrecked cars, mounting debt, health problems — we assume that we still only know about a third of what really went on with our own addicts.

As these behavioral symptoms present themselves, do not let your addict talk you out of what you know you see. For many of these behaviors, he will have a seemingly valid excuse. It's your job as the recovering enabler to know what you know and speak the truth. (But remember, it's not your job to fix anything.)

Addictive behavior symptoms in the order you are likely to witness them include:

- **Lying.** Though we covered this one pretty extensively in previous chapters, we cannot caution you enough here. As the addict's situation becomes more desperate, the dishonesty expands into stealing and worse. Actions that you never believed possible from your loved one, you will see the addict do. Do not underestimate how low the addict will go.
- **Blaming everyone else for his problems**. This telltale sign starts very early on the slippery slope of addiction. Whether it's an issue at work or burning the beans, it's always someone else's fault.
- **Hypochondria.** This is especially prevalent among drug addicts. They always have a disease that is hard to diagnose, but can be relieved with pain medication, (e.g., headaches, backaches, tooth pain). In my (Beth's) experience, the sad part is that many physicians — even if they have been alerted to the addiction — will give the addict painkillers just to get him out of their office. (More on this later.)

- **Disappearing for longer and longer periods of time**. Addicts just leave. And you don't know where they've gone. At first, they leave for a few hours and then it extends to days on end. Not all addicts do this, but don't let the behavior surprise you.
- **Loss of work.** Losing the ability to maintain a job is a red flag pointing to addiction. This symptom often goes hand in hand with the "blaming everyone else for his problems" symptom. If your addict loses his job, or a series of them, take it for what it is — an inability to function in the world. Don't allow the addict to convince you that this boss is just a jerk—no matter how much of a jerk his boss is.
- **Loss of daily function.** As the disease progresses, the addict loses his ability to participate in a normal life. No job. Smaller and smaller circle of friends. Unkempt surroundings. Unkempt appearance.
- **Broken everything.** No matter how clean a person your addict once was, your home and your possessions will deteriorate once the addiction takes hold. Wood surfaces will have rings. Furniture will be broken. Rugs will be stained. Walls will get chipped. Cars will get dented. And of course, nothing will get fixed.
- **Violence.** Needless to say, an addict's impulse-control knob doesn't work very well. In our experience, as they become more desperate they begin to act out with violence — even the ones who have never shown this tendency before. In addition to physical violence, they only speak to you to yell at you. It's the addiction lashing out, so don't take it personally. In fact, it would be best if you chose not to take it at all.
- **Increased TV watching.** None of our addicts were big television viewers before the addiction kicked into high gear. But as the disease progressed, all of them spent more and more time in front of the TV. In the end, across the board, the television was on 24/7.

By the way, as you begin to see these behaviors in the addict, it is also important that you take a good look in the mirror. Be honest about how many of these behaviors you — as an enabler — are displaying. As our enabling progresses, we allow our world to shrink, limiting our activities and friends because we have an addiction to take care of. We get angry at people who are trying to help us because they point out the truth of our situation and offer practical solutions. Our appearance deteriorates because we put self-care on the back burner. We blame outside forces — like drunk-driving laws — for our addict's problems. We blame our addict for our problems. (If he would just quit drinking, I'd be able to go to the gym and lose 20 pounds; you know you've thought that.) **Just as the addict gives his whole life over to the addictions, we enablers give our whole life over to the addict.**

Take Away:
The disease of addiction presents with
certain behaviors. Recognize them as part of the
disease that will infect you, the enabler, too.

Chapter 8:

In The End

As the addiction approaches the end — meaning that the addict approaches death — you may begin to think that you are dealing with someone with severe mental impairment. That's because you are. Alcohol and drugs — like any terminal illness — are poisons that stress the addict's organs, including the brain.

As the liver is taxed with alcohol and/or drugs, it becomes unable to clean the toxins from the system. So the poison is left in the blood stream and flows to the organs, eventually causing organ failure.

Ammonia brain

One of the more damaging of those toxins is ammonia, which is produced naturally in our digestive tract as proteins are broken down. In a healthy body, the liver converts that ammonia byproduct into urea, which then leaves the body. But when the liver is too taxed to do its job, the ammonia does not get converted and travels throughout the body. When it reaches the brain, the result can be hepatic encephalopathy — also known as "ammonia brain."

A person with ammonia brain has trouble sleeping, a short attention span, mood swings, problems with coordination ...sound familiar yet? Ultimately, with enough ammonia in their system, the person can fall into a coma. Pre-coma, the addict may start convulsing and throwing up blood on a regular basis. Not surprisingly, this condition can be fatal.

Hospital time

Obviously, when the addict is convulsing and throwing up blood, an ambulance is likely to be called, and, in our experience, the addict eventually ends up in the intensive care unit (ICU). There, the doctor is likely to tell you that this is the end. Be prepared that it just might be. But also be prepared that it might not be. We've had addicts who left the intensive care unit and continued to live in this desperate state for several years more. Others do indeed die.

Should your addict recover enough to be released from the hospital, you need to be prepared with a plan and boundaries around what you are willing to do and not do during this last (but sometimes long) stage of the disease.

We are conditioned to think that when a family member goes into the hospital, life stops and we must be there to serve. When the disease is addiction, we need to rethink this. Chances are good that your first go round in the ICU will be just that: the first of many. In fact, his hospitalization could become a regular routine. There is just no way to know.

So you have a choice to make. You can rush to the hospital every time your addict is admitted, giving up and ignoring the responsibilities in your life (your children, your job, yourself) and giving your life over to serving the addiction. Or you can draw some healthy boundaries. You can continue to go to work, care for your children, go to the gym, and go out with friends, and let the hospitalized addict fit into your schedule, if at all. **It's your choice**.

Be prepared for people to judge you for this. And for you to judge yourself at first. The truth is that your loved one is fine in the hospital — though the addiction itself is probably suffering somewhat. Your vigil will only add to his irritation and your resentment.

The hospital is going to release the addict quickly; hospitals are for providing acute care, not long-term care. Though a residential rehab program will most likely have been offered, don't bet on your addict taking the medical system up on this. Surprisingly, the patient cannot be forced into further treatment. Drinking or drugging yourself into the ICU isn't considered suicidal or mentally ill. (More on this later.)

Bottom line: It's up to you to decide on your boundaries once these hospital visits start. What are you willing to do (and "nothing" is a perfectly acceptable answer here if that's where you are) and what are you not willing to do. The lines you draw here are likely to change as time goes on and hospital admittances become part of the routine. The next chapters will give you some guidelines on what to expect and how to protect yourself.

> ### *Take Away:*
> *In the end, addiction compromises all organs, including the brain. Be prepared; the "last stages" of the disease can last years.*

Part Three: Managing Your Life

Chapter 9:

Protecting Yourself

As addiction marches through your life like Sherman's Army through the South, there are certain things you can do to limit the damage to yourself, your children and your finances, so that when you are ready to fully detach and reclaim your life, you have the resources to do so.

Journaling

This is not a diary of your feelings, though you can add them if you like. This is an account of the addict's actions. Remember "actions speak louder than words." This is your record of the addict's behavior to use for any future proceedings. We suggest using a written diary, writing in ink and dating your entries. Also, take photographs and video whenever possible.

- Write down and date events such as when he left the house high and got into a car, when and why he got arrested, when his words were not consistent with his actions, when and how he threatened you, when he stole from you, when he promised to get sober, how long he remained sober, etc.

- Take photographs of the addict living in filth, passed out in bed, visibly high at a family gathering, etc.
- Videotape him when he is high or drunk. Interview him and ask simple questions about his addiction, about his ability to live life, etc. Also videotape important events at which he is high.

Having this information in black and white — and living color — will serve as great evidence of the addict's condition should you need it for a divorce or custody hearing, or to obtain a restraining order.

It also gives you something tangible to look at and read in those moments when you feel pressure from the addict and don't know which way is up. You can read your entries and remember what this addiction has done to your loved one, to you and to your entire family. You can look at the truth of your life with addiction and from that gather the strength to detach yourself from it and starve the disease.

Legal and financial protection

Addicts go through money fast, rack up a lot of bills (as I'm sure you know) and cause property damage. The quicker you can untangle yourself from being legally liable for your addict's actions the better. (Remember parents are not responsible for an adult child!) Make an appointment with an attorney and ask how best to protect your assets from your addict.

If you are married to an addict, ask an attorney how to get as many assets as possible into your own name. If you are willing to leave or make your spouse leave the house, look into the laws in your state. Find out if getting a legal separation will eliminate your financially liability for your spouse, or if you need to file for a full divorce.

Your local women's shelter for victims of domestic violence can be a great resource here for finding a lawyer, creating a strategy for leaving and getting aid if you have no money. If you are going to have any chance, you must free yourself from legal liability here.

If you have reservations about getting separated or divorced, tell yourself what I (Beth) told myself. "I am doing this to protect our future. If he gets well, we can always get remarried. But to keep living like this is to keep digging my family into a financial and psychological hole." While I was married to my first husband, everything I earned went to support his addiction. We fed it before we fed ourselves. If he had killed someone while driving under the influence, we (myself and our son included) would have lost everything. With a divorce in hand, I was able to start building a life — I had a budget, bought a house, had a running car and insurance. Had he recovered and had I still wanted the marriage, that divorce would have meant that he had something to come home to as well. Without the divorce, the addiction would have destroyed us all.

As far as getting legal papers signed, we suggest that you use the few moments of sobriety that occur every now and then, when the addict's true personality comes back for a moment. Both our husbands could get angry when intoxicated. But when sober, both felt pretty guilty about their addiction. Use that guilt and those times to get important signatures.

Your own 911

If you choose not to leave, know that there will come a time when your addict becomes violent and you will need to leave. It does not matter docile he is now. As the disease progresses, so will his desperation. You need to have a plan for when that time comes.

- Keep gas in your car at all times.
- Keep cash and credit cards in your name for this purpose.
- Keep a bag packed with necessities, including medicines, contacts, glasses, etc.

- Know where you are going to go — if you are planning to stay with friends or relatives, be sure that they know your plan.

Take Away:
You can take steps now to protect yourself and your assets from the addiction.

Chapter 10:

Protecting Your Children

Just like everyone knows your addict is an addict, your children know too. And if they don't know, they need to.

What do you tell the kids?

We are not trained psychologists. But as children of an alcoholic and an enabler, we say don't lie to your children because it messes with their heads and their ability to believe in their own inner compass. And without that ability to listen to their gut, they will grow to dismiss behaviors (as they've been taught to do) and make bad choices where people are concerned.

A friend of ours who also grew up in an alcoholic family put it this way: **"As a little girl, it was like I kept telling everyone that the sky was blue. And they would say 'no, no, dear, the sky is green.' I knew something was wrong with my father, but the adults I trusted kept telling me that I was wrong. And so, I didn't know what to think or who to believe."**

Healthy detachment from the addict will help you to help your children. You do not need to be angry with the addict. The addiction is the interloper here, and the children should understand that. At the same time, your children need to know that it is not safe to be with the addicted relative. He is sick, and his judgment cannot be trusted.

Tell them: (Daddy, Mommy, Uncle Joe, Aunt Sally, whoever) loves them, but that he is not well. Tell them that his disease makes him say and do unsafe things. Ask them to be aware of this. Explain that he would never want to hurt them, but that he can't think right because of the disease. Ask them to call you immediately if they ever feel unsure or if they are left alone with him. Tell them never to get in a car with the addict. And tell them that you're doing everything you can to make the addict well again.

Obviously, if you have teenagers, you can explain more and let them know that they are no longer dealing with a responsible adult. The addict's judgment is not to be trusted. That is not to say that we are unloving or unsupportive; that is to speak and deal in truth. The addict is poisoning his or her brain and not thinking clearly. **Also, be sure that your teenagers know this is NOT their fault and that it is NOT within their power to make it better.**

As parents, it is our responsibility to keep our children away from the addict. But should our child come into contact with an active addict, it is our responsibility to call a spade a spade and model correct behavior. "Uncle John is under the influence right now. He is not himself. We are leaving."

If you do separate or divorce, do not allow unsupervised visitation between your children and your addict— even if he goes into rehab. This is where your journal will come in handy. It gives you something to show a judge the truth of the situation. It's up to you, the sober adult, to make sure your child is safe. Would you let the addiction watch your child? Then don't let the addict — recovering or not.

However, understand that the legal system has to do the "legal" thing. We know of many cases where judges order unsupervised visitation between addicts and their children. They order that addicts must be sober to pick up their children and remain sober while they have them. Yeah right. That order is about as useful as a restraining order in protecting children. Your addict might (and that's a big might) be sober when he picks them up, but do we really have any faith that an addict is going to remain that way throughout the visit. And are we willing to risk our children's lives and mental health on his sobriety. Under no circumstance, no matter how sober he appears, should an addict be allowed to have your children in his car or in his care. If you are given such a decree, you might want to ask the judge if he would leave his children with your addict. (Again, use your journal in court.)

That said, consider keeping your children safe by keeping the courts out of it if possible. Don't turn custody into a contest. If possible, work with your addict to provide safe, sober, supervised visits that relieve his guilt and keep your children safe. I (Beth) took my son to see his father whenever his dad was sober. We visited together as a family. It was nice because I got to temporarily visit with my sober husband and my son had his father for a few hours every few weeks. However, when I returned home from those visits, I would read my journal and look at the photographs of how we had been living so that I didn't fall back into magical thinking. Eventually, my husband stopped calling because he was unable to have a sober day.

> ### *Take away:*
> ### *Tell your children the truth with love and compassion for the addict.*

Chapter 11:

Outside Help Is Not That Available

Though addiction is a very common problem, with widespread consequences for society at large, our social safety nets – human services, medical services and legal services – here in the U.S. are not set up to deal with addiction and its many issues. Personally, we think the help isn't there because addiction problems are multi-faceted, with no clear resolution. It's messy and frustrating. Thus, for the most part, even when you ask for help, you may not find it. Be prepared to deal with the fallout of addiction on your own. However, there will be times when your addict does end up in part of the system and from our experience, this is what you can expect:

The medical community at large

If you've watched HBO's wonderful documentary *Addiction*, then you know that there are some very exciting breakthroughs taking place in the medical treatment of addiction. If you've seen the television shows *Celebrity Rehab* or *Intervention*, then you know that there are gorgeous treatment centers with waiting therapists throughout the United States.

Unfortunately, most addicts — yours included — won't have access to a physician who offers those breakthrough treatments. And your addict probably can't afford a residential rehab program, which can cost anywhere from $5,000 a month to well over $80,000 a month. (The majority of residential treatment programs fall in the $20,000-a-month range.) Even if the addict does have insurance and it will pay for residential treatment, the program is usually a 28-day program. This may or may not be enough time for your addict to set a foundation for sobriety.

Physicians

Obviously, addicts are going to have health problems. (And some feign illness so they can get drugs.) Though addiction/alcoholism is common, for some reason, in our experience, most physicians don't pick up on an addiction as the possible root issue. So don't be surprised if your addict's physician doesn't recognize the addiction, isn't up on the latest addiction research and, in fact, completely ignores the addiction as he treats your addict for whatever complaint.

For instance, our brother Ted went to the doctor because he couldn't sleep — a common, well-known side-effect of alcoholism. We think anyone familiar with alcoholism could have seen that Ted was a severe alcoholic just by looking at him. But the doctor ordered that Ted go to the sleep lab to test for sleep apnea instead of dealing with the addiction.

Telling doctors or emergency room nurses that your loved one has an addiction is no guarantee that they will stop prescribing. Some do. Some don't. I (Beth) always told physicians that my husband was addicted to painkillers, but many of them kept prescribing the pills despite my pleas. Some physicians do care and will thank you for informing them. Always tell the addict's physician and give them a chance to do the right thing.

Treatment centers

If you are lucky and your addict agrees to go into treatment and has a way to pay for it, he still has to find a treatment center. Finding an effective program can be like finding a needle in a haystack. There are more than 13,000 treatment centers in the United States. And according to the HBO documentary *Addiction*, there are "no published standards for effective addiction treatment."

Because of insurance, most programs offer 30-day inpatient treatment and 90-day outpatient treatment. A family program is usually part of the treatment, but most of the care focuses on the addict.

Our personal experience with rehabilitation centers has not been good. Our first intervention was with our father in the mid-1980s. He agreed to treatment and was there for three days or so before he left.

Both of our husbands entered different programs at different times. Both finished the 28-day, inpatient part of their programs. Both relapsed within weeks (maybe days, we don't really know) of coming home. In both cases, the family part of the therapy consisted of a few group meetings; nothing that really addressed where we as spouses were emotionally or what we could expect. As I (Beth) recall, no one prepared me for relapse. Neither of our husbands made it through the entire 90 days of outpatient therapy.

My (Beth's) poor husband never had a chance. During his outpatient treatment, the program's psychiatrist — touted as an addiction specialist at a major university hospital — prescribed my opiate-addicted husband 90 purple Xanax a month and instructed me to dole them out to him. This fueled both my husband's addiction and my enabling. (Xanax is a benzodiazepine, a downer.) At the time, I didn't know any better. In retrospect, that's a lot of incompetence for a $20,000 price tag.

So if your addict wants to go to a treatment center, he needs to do some research before committing his money and his life, which right there seems like an incredible hurdle for an addict.

FYI: A list of treatment centers can be found on the website of the Substance Abuse and Mental Health Services Administration, which is part of the U.S. Department of Health and Human Services (http://findtreatment.samhsa.gov). The centers listed are licensed but not rated and offer all levels of programming.

In our opinion, a good program would offer:

- **Inpatient treatment that lasts at least 90 days**
- **An in-depth family program that really explores the relationship between enabling and addiction**
- **Opportunity for assessment and treatment for dual diagnosis — addiction often accompanies other mental disorders, such as depression, anxiety, etc.**
- **Realistic outcomes — on average, 40 to 60 percent of patients relapse after rehab. A good center should acknowledge this and offer programming and support for managing addiction for life.**
- **Referrals from patients and their families.**

New evidence suggests some success with forced treatment for addiction and addicts do not have to reach "their bottom" before seeking help. However, before you start making plans to find and pay for rehab for your addict, you should know that the research also finds that at some point, for treatment to work, **the patient must still become responsible for his own recovery**. In addition, most treatment centers don't accept patients against their will. And if your addict is an adult, you need a legal way to force him into recovery (*see our section on the legal system*).

Most importantly, before you take this responsibility from your addict, ask yourself why you feel the need to do this. Examine your motives and expectations, and take full responsibility for the actions you choose to take, or not take, in the end. If you do oversee his placement in rehab and his recovery isn't sustained (and most aren't on the first attempt), don't blame your addict. After all, this was your plan, not his.

Hospitals

Since treatment centers are not a likely option for most people, your addict will eventually end up in the emergency room and then in the hospital. As we discussed earlier, hospitals are for acute care. They are not set up to handle treatment for addiction, though most addicts land there.

Once physically stabilized, the hospitalized addict will be asked if he wants to enter a treatment program. If he says no — and most addicts say no — then he will be released back out into the world and sent a bill. This dangerous and expensive pattern will continue until the addict either decides to enter treatment or dies.

Several months before his suicide, our brother Ted was released from a three-day stay in the intensive care unit of our local hospital. We asked the psychiatrist who released him what criteria was used to determine that our brother was stable enough to be back in the community. The psychiatrist said he offered our brother rehab and Ted refused, so there was nothing he, the psychiatrist, could do. We argued that our brother was unstable and violent and had access to a car and guns. Wasn't there somewhere we could put him in order to keep him, our mother and our community safe? The answer was no.

Unfortunately and rather unbelievably, you cannot commit an addict. Which leads us to the legal system.

The legal system

To commit someone, he must be a threat to himself or others. For some reason, addicts do not meet these criteria in the eyes of the law. Obviously, someone who drinks so much alcohol that he ends up in intensive care is a threat to himself. Obviously, when that same person is released to get behind the wheel of a car (which they do when you release them from the hospital), he is a threat to the community. Obviously, that is, unless you are in addiction limbo — caught somewhere between the legal and medical systems.

I (Meridith) went to our local magistrate to commit my first husband. His eyes and skin were yellow, he had not been sober or out of bed for weeks, and I thought he was going to die. So the police came and got him and took him to the hospital to see if he could be committed. At the hospital, they observed him and released him back to me after a few hours, saying he would not agree to enter treatment and that he was not a threat to himself. They told me that there was nothing they could do.

While still living on his own in Maryland, before moving in with our mother, our brother Ted wrote a detailed suicide note and had a gun. We called the suicide hot line. They told us that they couldn't help unless he went to a mental health facility on his own. They suggested that we call the police to get him to a hospital. The police came and took him to the hospital. There, a physician asked Ted if he was a threat to himself (one look at him would have told you yes, plus the evidence of the suicide note). Ted said no. So the hospital released him and sent him a bill for $900.

After his most recent — and last — stay in our local ICU, the hospital's psychiatrist released Ted, saying that he wasn't a threat to himself or others. Once released, Ted went back to our mother's home and continued to steal tens of thousands of dollars from her; drove through our town drunk every day; was eventually arrested for drunk driving and continued to drive; harassed and frightened a neighbor to the point that she took out a restraining order; and eventually shot himself in our mother's presence. As horrible as that day was, we just thank the stars that he didn't shoot our mother or some other innocent person hiking the trail behind her house.

Before depression and alcoholism took over his life, Ted was a highly respected professional in the technology industry and had a very good salary. Throughout his life, until the end, he was noted for his intellect and extremely dry wit. He was also a great cook.

In all these years of dealing with addiction, we have learned that the police do come when you call. And they are great at making you and your addict safe for the moment. But the rest of the system has its hands tied when it comes to getting the addict somewhere where he can get help before he seriously hurts someone. Until this changes (and not much has changed since we began dealing with our dad in the 1980s), you are pretty much on your own.

Take Away:
Be prepared; our medical and legal systems are not structured to help with the issues created by addiction.

Part Four: Living

Chapter 12:

Your Recovery

When you live with an addict, the last thing on your list is you. You are so busy taking care of him, so busy being distracted by the drama, pain and chaos of your life, that there is no room to take care of yourself or even look at your own behavior. In some ways, like your addict, you slowly go crazy. You slip so slowly that you don't even notice it. Until one day (again like your addict) you are a mere fraction of the person you used to be. That is when you reach your bottom—and it's time for your recovery.

Ten years into my (Meridith's) relationship with my alcohol-addicted husband, he said the words that would spark my recovery, the words that would save my life. To this day, I believe that this was the most loving thing he ever said to me. We were fighting, yet again. I was working two jobs just to make ends meet and keep a roof over our heads, and I came home to find another maxed-out credit card bill and an empty vodka bottle. I snapped, just like I had done so many times before. I am sure, looking back, that I was sad, hurt and a whole range of other emotions, but at that time in my life, I believe the only feeling I had anymore was anger.

Each time this happened (and it happened more times than I care to remember), I would go into a fit of anger and start screaming at the top of my lungs, asking how he could do this to me and whether he realized how hard I worked, what I had done for him to keep a roof over his head, clothes on his back, his bills paid and his credit clean. This time he did not fight back. He just looked at me, listened to me and with a calm, controlled voice he uttered these important words — "You are a f***ing lunatic; who asked you to?"

And while I am sure he had screamed those words at me before, for some reason this time he was calm, this time he was even-tempered, and this time it resonated with me and a light bulb went off. At that moment I woke up and I realized he was right. I was a f***ing lunatic and no one — not even him — had asked me to do all the things I had done "for him."

I realized then that I had been so obsessed with his disease that I could not see my own. You see, he had NEVER asked me to work hard, feed him, pay his bills or keep his credit clean. Those were decisions I made, choices I made every day about how and on whom to spend my time, my money and my energy.

Beyond that, I realized that even if he had asked me to do all of those things, it wouldn't have mattered. It finally became clear to me that **the choices I was making in my life were mine and mine alone to make**. And if I was honest with myself, the person I was so angry with was not my husband — not the addict in my life — but me. It became clear to me that my life was miserable — just like my addict's — simply because I chose for it to be that way. **Just like he was throwing it all away for a bottle of vodka, I was throwing it all away trying to save an addict.**

That was the day I, thank god, hit bottom. That was the day I headed back to Al-Anon (after having been six or eight times before), and that was the time it stuck. That was the time the message got through and my life began to change for the better. My addict did not recover, but I did. Ironically, I could not save his life, but it was his words that saved mine.

The truth is no one "recovers" from anything in life until they are ready. Just like we made the choices to mess our lives up, we have to make the choices to get back on the right track. No one can do it for us, no one can force us to make that decision, and no one can make the path to recovery easy. However, once we do make the decision, it does take others to help us get there.

Saying "no more" is merely the beginning. You must realize that you have years of habits, patterns and comfort zones to break. So where do you start?

You know you need help, so now is the time to get some

Remember that you can't do everything by yourself — especially when it comes to changing entrenched behaviors. Tough words for an enabler, we know. Here are some support systems to consider as you begin working your way through recovery:

- **Al-Anon (Find a meeting www.al-anon.org)**
  This is the single most important resource we recommend. The lessons these meetings hold about personal responsibility can change anyone's life for the better—whether or not you are dealing with an addict. Shop around for meetings. Find someone there you can relate to, where you can see your situation reflected in another's life. And don't worry if what is said seems like a bunch of hooey at first; keep going, keep listening and you'll begin to take in the concepts that Al-Anon teaches and use them to take charge of your life.

- **Therapy**
  If you choose to go this route, and both of us have over the years, choose a therapist who knows addiction through life experience. You can read all the books you want and study all the theories, but until you've lived it, you can't understand it.

In your first interview, ask outright if they have had personal experience with addiction. And of course, also check licensing and references and get referrals — as you would with any professional you hire.

- ### Friends and family
  Surrounding yourself with the people who love and support not only you, but also what you are trying to do, is critical to your recovery. Really look at who you have in your life vs. who you need in your life. In the beginning you are fragile, and you need people who want to see you succeed, and who don't judge you for the changes you make or the slips you may have. You need people who will be honest with you, hold you accountable and shoot straight with you about your lying, judgment and overall guilt and anger.

When I (Meridith) made the decision to seek help, two of the biggest obstacles I had to get over were changing the people in my life and coming to terms with my "dark side." When I began to put my own needs and wants above that of the addict, both my mother and my mother-in-law were two of my biggest obstacles. My (by this time widowed) mother loved my husband, and she had this picture in her mind of a strong, capable and loving man. She felt that I would struggle without him and to some degree felt that I owed him for all he had done for me. My mother-in-law felt that I was the reason for her son's addiction; if I were just nicer, more supportive and home more, then none of this would have become a problem.

Limiting my time with both of them was key to my recovery. In the beginning I was consumed with guilt, personal judgment and a need for comfort. Any reason to go back to the way things had been would set me off. For the first year of recovery, limiting my time with both my mother and mother-in-law meant the difference between success and failure.

Instead, I increased the amount of time I spent with my sister, Al-Anon and those few friends who were open to listening to what I was going through. These people would laugh with me about what I was feeling and would hold me accountable for making changes and taking personal responsibility for my life. In other words, I needed people who would not let me whine when I refused to own my situation and make the needed changes.

Our advice would be to explore all the support systems you can but not to get stuck in any one. Take what you find in each that resonates with you and helps you grow more confident in yourself. To be successful in your recovery, you must also be willing to:

- **Take responsibility**
  Understand that your choices are yours and yours alone. Look at your life and decide what you love about it and what you don't, and what you can and cannot change. Believe that you are where you are — good and bad — because you decided for some reason to put yourself there.

- **Accept reality**
  Part of recovery is accepting what we cannot change. So much of the reason we wind up in the situation we are in is simply because we keep trying to change what we cannot control. Look at your life and the people in it, and accept the reality of your life.

- **Take action**
  Take the steps you need to get the help and support you need, so you know what to change and how to change it. Join an Al-Anon group, read books, find supportive friends and/or family, and even a sponsor.

- **Change behaviors**
  Once you have the information you need to know what and how to change, you have to commit to change. This is not easy. It takes self-awareness, practice and perseverance. For instance, the next time someone asks you to volunteer for something or

do something, before you answer, take a deep breath, count to three, and say, "No." (You can always say yes later if you really want to.) But being in the practice of saying "no" first can become a powerful tool in your evolution.

- **Grant forgiveness – of yourself**

  As you go through this change, you take one step forward and two steps back. You need to understand that this is a daily struggle. Certainly it gets easier with each day and each situation. Know that you will find your way and that you will get stronger with the more compassion you show to yourself, and the more you forgive yourself. Be generous to yourself for each struggle you have and each wrong decision you make.

- **Practice self-awareness**

  The only way to grow and to change your behaviors is to learn to be aware of yourself, to connect your mind and your actions. You must take note of what you do. Ask yourself why you do it and what it feels like in your body when you do it. Don't judge yourself but get honest with the answers. Connecting mind and body will help you learn about yourself. Decide what you truly want and what you truly don't.

- **Listen to yourself**

  Figure out what you want in and out of life, not what everyone else wants for you or thinks you should do. Learn that happiness in life is yours and yours alone to decide on and to choose.

Take Away:
It's time to take care of yourself, not the addiction. Find solid support and start work on your recovery.

Chapter 13:

The Good Stuff

What recovery brings you

Once you break free of the chains of addiction, you win big, and you get a prize that is the greatest of all. A prize that keeps on giving and expanding. The prize is your life.

And as you begin your recovery, you will realize that this wonderful prize is something you have not seen or experienced in many years. You will be so happy to have this prize that you will wonder how you ever managed without it. Every step you take in your recovery gives you more and more of your life back.

You gain:

- *Compassion*
  You find compassion for yourself and the addicts in your life, and yes, you *can* find compassion for the addicts in your life. This is so important. As compassion comes into your life, anger

goes out. While there will still be pain, you will also feel a sense of calmness and healthy love for the addicts in your life.

- *Acceptance*
  You begin to realize that everyone, including you, was doing the best they could at the time. You realize that we are all just learning and growing following our own path … that makes us human.

- *Boundaries*
  You gain the ability to set limits in your life with both people and perceived responsibilities. You learn to say no to unwanted projects and people. You learn to say yes to the activities and the people you want in your life.

- *Peace*
  You gain a life almost free of guilt. You live in truth. No more secrets. No more hiding. Your intentions are pure. Your life is an open book.

- *Joy*
  Joy returns to your life. You let go of the anger, guilt and weight of other people's lives, and replace it with the joy of your own life. You'll notice a light heartedness in your attitude, a smile on your face and kindness in your actions.

- *Hope*
  Your dreams will return. You become clear about what you want, and you find the courage to go after it.

- *Your life*
  The biggest difference is that you stop living for the future and start living for the now. You stop thinking that you will do things

next year and be happy next year. You live life understanding that the time to live is now.

Obviously, recovery from addiction and enabling doesn't happen overnight. It's a process. A process we have been actively working on for 15 years or more and suppose we will be working on the rest of our lives. No, we are not expecting any more addicts to appear in our lives. But our enabling behaviors continue to appear under the guise of kindness — keeping a supplier on who is not doing his job, spending time with people we don't like, over volunteering our time to the detriment of our families and ourselves, etc., etc., etc.

You've heard of alcoholics having dry-drunk behavior. Well, even when our lives are free of addicts, we enablers continue to find ways to stunt emotional growth in others and ourselves by "just taking care of it ourselves" whenever we can. Recovery is forever for the enabler — but the enabling becomes easier to identify and catch and the learning curve lessens.

In fact, when you choose to forge ahead in your own recovery, you will be surprised at how quickly life improves. That is not to say that changing your behavior is easy or that moments of great anxiety don't appear, and it is not to say that addiction won't continue to try you, because it will. But once you catch on to detachment and begin to take personal responsibility for your actions, managing life becomes almost immediately easier.

As you become stronger and more confident on the inside, your outer life automatically becomes a reflection of that. If you deem it so, **a realized life is the silver lining waiting to appear from the cloud of addiction.** Go for it — and go find an Al-Anon group.

Take Away:
You will not only survive addiction; you will thrive because of addiction. And that's the straight dope!

Afterword

Like all novice authors, we had professional associates and friends read this book before we went to publication. One question that kept popping up was where are we (Beth and Meridith) today. Do we drink? Do drugs? Are we happy? What's next for our lives?

After years of therapy, tons of reading, lots of painful soul searching, and miles and miles of talking on the hiking trail, both of us are living rather peaceful lives, void of big drama. Both of us are married again — though it took a lot of therapy and dating before we found ourselves attracted to men who didn't "need us." After a lifetime of being the "good one" and taking care of everything, it is revealing, humbling, unbelievably frustrating, and some kind of wonderful to be part of equal partnerships between adults and to be able to trust our partners to be the caretakers sometimes.

We both feel, however, that we are still works in progress. We are without active addicts in our lives, but that doesn't mean that we've given up enabling. We both continue to enable whenever we get the chance, especially during times of stress. (A hint for you: When you see yourself trying to direct another adult's life or saying "yes" to things you don't want to do, your enabling has reared its head.)

I (Beth) do drink alcohol. I like to have wine in the evenings while my husband and I cook. So obviously I don't mind other people drinking. However, people who consume a lot of alcohol continue to make me abnormally anxious. I find myself becoming fixated on their behavior whether or not I know them, and I am unable to enjoy myself. My husband and I go out to hear live music quite often. Occasionally, I have had to leave a venue because someone or a group of people was visibly intoxicated, causing my anxiety level to go through the roof.

I (Meridith) do not drink and never really have. My drugs of choice have always been food, work and structure. My issues with food and structure are now somewhat under control, but I remain to this day a workaholic. My husband does drink and enjoys a glass of wine or a beer after work, which doesn't bother me at all. Most of my friends drink, and I can honestly say that I have never had an issue with their choice to do so, although many have asked. To this day, however, the abuse of alcohol or addictive behaviors makes me anxious, and I tend to remove myself from those situations. I choose not to be around people who abuse alcohol, and I do not have friends or choose to work with anyone who relies heavily on drugs (prescription or illegal).

While those are the most obvious scars left from a life surrounded by addiction, the more aware I become of my own actions and behaviors the more I have noticed some smaller, kind of quirky scars that still play a very big role in my life. I get extremely anxious when I am around people who say unkind things about friends or family and then are kind when in their presence. Living with addicts, I have been lied to so much, that I am extremely uncomfortable in relationships that are not completely transparent or authentic.

Then there is my constant need for reassurance. My poor husband tolerates the fact that when I am traveling, I have a high need to be in touch. Tragedy has struck those I love so often that I need a quick text, voicemail message or a quick call every day just to be sure he is happy and healthy. While many of these issues have been with me and will be with me for life, the difference now is that I am aware they are my issues, and I feel no need to judge them. Perhaps one day, I will be able to "outgrow" them, but for now just understanding and accepting them has been enough. My commitment to self-awareness allows me to continue to make choices without judgment of myself or others.

Neither of us smokes pot or takes pills — or ever really did, to any great extent. I (Beth) went along with the crowd in high school and college (child of the 70s). But ultimately, I didn't like the feeling of being out of control, I hate not feeling my best in the morning, and I have always been too cheap to spend money on drugs. We both, however, have had and still have issues about food, but that's a whole other book.

We have no idea why addiction seems to strike the men in our family, while the women are infected with enabling. That's a question for science.

An upside to a lifetime of dealing with addicts is that we have become rather fearless when it comes to life's challenges. The advice we've put forth in this book about dealing with an addict is advice that we continue to use every day in our businesses, our social relationships and our lives. Whatever life throws at us, we simply return to the basics:

1. Is it a problem for me?
2. Actions speak louder than words
3. Coddling a behavior encourages the behavior
4. We are responsible for what we choose to do
5. We —and what we want — matter

For instance, when I (Beth) began dating again after my divorce and years of therapy, I realized that I preferred having specific information — date and time — for going out. When I was younger, I never would have acknowledged this need. I wouldn't have wanted to be any trouble to anyone. I would simply have allowed my date to set ground rules. But as a recovering enabler, I became unafraid to recognize that I like specifics and that not having specifics was a **problem for me** and **that mattered**. Acting as if I didn't mind not knowing what the plans were until the last minute (i.e., **coddling that behavior)** only encouraged it. So, because **I was responsible** for what I agreed to, I let go of the freewheelers (I did not try to change them) and dated guys who called with specific plans. The result was that I began spending time with people who were better suited to me. And the freewheelers were better off too. They were no longer dating someone (me) who would have become very passive-aggressive around their spontaneity.

As an independent contractor who depends on billable hours for my living, I (Meridith) recently stopped agreeing to casually meeting people for lunch. At first, I was almost frightened to do this. I thought it sounded harsh (that was my enabler needing to be needed). But an hour lunch just to chat took at least two hours out of my workday. **It was a problem for me.** Those unbilled hours took time away from my paying customers and my family, **which mattered to me.** Ultimately, **I was responsible** for agreeing to the lunches. So I stopped agreeing. And I gave myself back that time to spend on pursuits and people that were important to me.

The long road of addiction that life has forced us to walk has beaten us down to the ground and brought us back up to a more intimate and deliberate existence on this earth. It has made us understand the value of being as open as we can be, unafraid to ask tough questions, able to listen to hard truths and glad to take full responsibility for where we are and where we are going. And honestly, we've found that it's the only way to really live.

Take Aways

Chapter 1: You have a problem. You are the solution.

Chapter 2: Your enabling behaviors encourage the addiction.

Chapter 3: The more you enable, the further from recovery you push your addict. Draw and adhere to compassionate boundaries.

Chapter 4: When someone speaks a hard truth, listen.

Chapter 5: Actions speak louder than words.

Chapter 6: If you want to stop your dance with addiction, you, the enabler, must leave the floor. We are not victims. We are responsible for our choices.

Chapter 7: The disease of addiction presents with certain behaviors. Recognize them as part of the disease that will infect you, the enabler, too.

Chapter 8: In the end, addiction compromises all organs, including the brain. Be prepared; the "last stages" of the disease can last years.

Chapter 9: You can take steps now to protect yourself and your assets from the addiction.

Chapter 10: Tell your children the truth with love and compassion for the addict.

Chapter 11: Be prepared; our medical and legal systems are not structured to help with the issues created by addiction.

Chapter 12: It's time to take care of yourself, not the addiction. Find solid support and start work on your recovery.

Chapter 13: You will not only survive addiction; you will thrive because of addiction. And that's the straight dope!

Resources

Al-Anon

A support group for codependents based on the 12-step program. Meetings are available in just about every community throughout the world, at no cost. In addition to the meetings, these groups also offer a great library of books and pamphlets.
www.al-anon.org

Addiction

This 2007 HBO documentary provides the most thorough explanation of the disease of addiction that we've found. The nation's foremost experts on addiction discuss the disease, the latest research and the latest treatments. The piece also features patients struggling with addiction and their families. In addition to the film itself, the documentary's website offers great information and resources.
http://www.hbo.com/addiction/

The Real Dope on Dealing with an Addict Website

A companion to this book, our website offers a variety of supports to help you in your journey to reclaim your life. On it, you'll find a community forum to share thoughts and experiences, and our blog with the latest information and resources for codependents like us. www.dealingwithanaddict.com

33397817R00061

Made in the USA
Lexington, KY
23 June 2014